HISTORY AS EVIDENCE
ANCIENT
GREECE

JOHN ELLIS JONES
Illustrated by David Salariya and Shirley Willis

Warwick Press

Contents

Editor: Caroline Royds
Designer: Ben White

The Publishers wish to thank the following for supplying photographs for this book: 9 *top* J. Ellis Jones; 19 *top* Deutsches Archaeologisches Institut, Athens; 20 J. Ellis Jones; 22–23 J. Ellis Jones; 26 *top* Alison Frantz, *bottom* Michael Holford, 27 *top* Alison Frantz, *bottom left* Ronald Sheridan; 28 *top* ZEFA; 30 *center* J. Ellis Jones; 32 J. Ellis Jones; 34 J. Ellis Jones.

Published 1983 by Warwick Press,
387 Park Avenue South, New York, New York 10016

First published in Great Britain by
Kingfisher Books Limited 1983.

Copyright © Kingfisher Books Ltd 1983.

Printed in Italy by Vallardi Industrie Grafiche, Milan.

6 5 4 3 2 1 All rights reserved

ISBN 0-531-09220-8

Below: Greece is a land of high mountains, small valleys and plains, with a coastline broken by many peninsulas and gulfs, and with numerous islands. It was open to influences by land and sea, but difficult to unite into one great state. In ancient times it had many small city-states, each with its own territory. Some, like Athens, Sparta and Corinth became famous, and won control for a time over others. In the 5th century BC, Sparta and her allies dominated the Peloponnese, while Athens formed the Aegean coastal states into a short-lived empire.

Sparta & her allies
Athenian domination
Persian Empire
Unaligned areas

Introduction

This book is about the peoples of ancient Greece. Their civilization stretched over more than a thousand years and, during that time, changed a great deal. From the archaeological remains – of cities, houses, temples and streets – we can build up a picture of life at different periods in their history.

The first site chosen here, Mycenae, developed very early in Greek history, in the prehistoric period – that is in the time before people kept any written records of their activities. It is a royal citadel or stronghold of the Bronze Age (2500–1000 BC). The next two sites, the city of Athens and the sanctuary of Olympia, had their roots in that age, but did not become really important places until the early historical or ARCHAIC period (800–500 BC) and the CLASSICAL period which followed (500–300 BC). The last site, the island of Delos, was well-known as a sanctuary in archaic and classical times, but reached its peak of prosperity later, in the HELLENISTIC period (300–150 BC). It continued to flourish after that, when Greece had become a province of the Roman Empire.

Below: Ancient Greece corresponded in size to the modern state of Greece, but Greek peoples lived outside that area too. Settlers from the mainland (orange) spread and colonized many other parts of the Mediterranean (beige), setting up similar city-states to those at home (750–500 BC). The map shows several colonial cities. Many in Asia Minor, Sicily and Italy became powerful. Those in the west very much influenced the development of the Etruscans and the Romans in Italy. Later, after Alexander, King of Macedon (336–323 BC), had conquered the Near East, Greek influences and settlers spread even further (yellow).

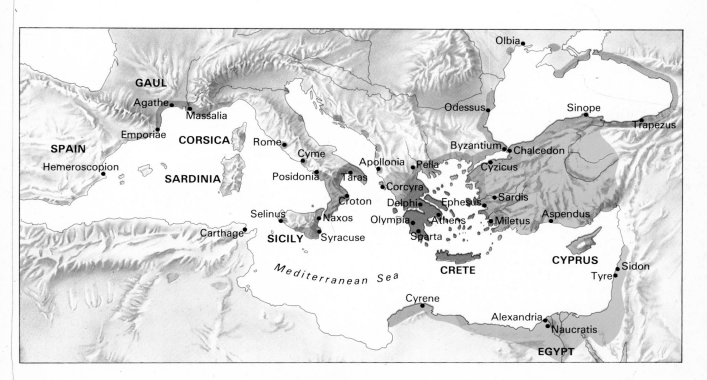

Mycenae

At Mycenae in southern Greece lie the ruins of an ancient citadel. It is a good place to begin finding out about the lives of the early Greeks, for the remains uncovered there are part of the little evidence we have about people who lived before history was written, or any records kept.

Mycenae is an inland site in the Peloponnese, the southern part of Greece which is divided from the north by the narrow Gulf of Corinth. The ruins there are clearly those of a powerful Bronze Age state, a fortress, a palace, a royal seat. The citadel sits on a hill, perched between two higher peaks. It controls the passes northwards towards Corinth and commands long views south to the sea across a fertile plain – past other ancient fortresses at Argos, Tiryns and Nauplion. All four citadels were well placed to dominate the plain and to resist attack, but classical legends, some 700 years later, told of a time when the kings of Mycenae had been masters of the whole region, and much of Greece besides. Their fortunes are very different today. Argos and Nauplion are prosperous towns, while Tiryns and Mycenae are only ancient monuments.

In 1876, a German merchant turned archaeologist called Heinrich Schliemann began excavating at Mycenae. Just inside the Lion Gate, he discovered five deep and undisturbed tombs in a royal cemetery. They lay inside a round double fence of stone slabs, the so-called Grave Circle A. Above them had stood upright tombstones carved with spiral patterns and

Above: In the late Bronze Age (1500–1200 BC), Mycenae was the center of a kingdom and at the height of its power. The map also shows other important citadels and palaces of Mycenaean times on the mainland. In the *Iliad*, the poet Homer tells of the destruction of far distant Troy by Agamemnon, King of Mycenae, and his army of Greeks. The island of Crete was the home of the earlier Minoan civilization, named after the legendary Cretan king, Minos.

Right: The Lion Gate, main entrance of the citadel of Mycenae. This is how the German Heinrich Schliemann, the first excavator of Mycenae, illustrated it in his book *Mycenae and Tiryns* in 1878. The Lion Gate, four metres wide and high, was big enough for carts to go through. It was framed by four huge stone slabs, the side pillars having several holes for the bars which bolted the two doors in place. Above the gateway was a thinner slab carved with lions supporting a pillar. Originally the lions' faces were masks of colored stone or gilded bronze pegged into holes in the stone slab. The lions were a symbol of the royal power of the kings of Mycenae.

Left: A view of the citadel of Mycenae from the west, showing the outer walls which have been restored in recent years. The royal palace was built on a hill between two mountain peaks, defended by slopes, and a deep ravine on one side. The great fortification wall lower down the hill was made of massive boulders fitted together. This style of building is called Cyclopean, after a legendary family of giants, the Cyclopes, who were said to have built the fortifications. The gateways were constructed of squared stone slabs.

scenes, two of which included warriors and horse-drawn chariots. The tombs below were pits lined with stone and roofed with slabs, but the slabs had long fallen in by the time they were uncovered. Inside, Schliemann found the skeletons of men, women and children, fifteen altogether, buried in rich garments decorated with gold. Five had gold masks over the face, and each was surrounded by personal treasures: gold and silver goblets, cups, flagons, vases, diadems, necklaces, pendants, rings, inlaid swords and daggers. When one of the masks was lifted, Schliemann could see the dried, crumpled features of the face below. He had it painted by a local artist, and later published an engraving of the drawing.

Schliemann believed he had found the remains of Agamemnon, King of Mycenae, and his friends, who were murdered by his queen Clytemnaestra and his cousin Aegisthus. Their story is associated with the conquering king's return from the Trojan War, dated by Greek tradition to early in the 12th century BC.

Other Greek and British archaeologists have since excavated at Mycenae. They have added a sixth tomb to Grave Circle A and have dated all six tombs to the 16th century BC, and the enclosing circle itself to the 12th century, after the Lion Gate and the western part of the fortress wall were built. They have also revealed an underground well-chamber in another late extension of the walls at the east end, and uncovered many of the internal buildings of the palace on the summit. Outside the walls, they discovered a second and even earlier Grave Circle (B), and cleared nine large royal tombs of a different type, called beehive tombs, set into the hillsides. They have also excavated the chamber-tombs and houses of some of the prosperous inhabitants of the town outside the citadel. This evidence has given us a much fuller picture of Mycenae itself and of the late Bronze Age.

Above: With other treasures from the royal tombs, Schliemann found this golden cup, shown above as he found and illustrated it in 1878, and below as it has been restored. The poet Homer described just such a cup, with pigeons perched on the handles, being used by the hero Nestor in his tent before Troy.

The Citadel

Right: A reconstruction of the citadel of Mycenae from the same viewpoint as the photograph on the previous page. The royal palace on the hilltop was built on different levels, with terraces, staircases, and a number of rooms grouped around the high hall, the "Megaron". This had a porch with columns, an inner porch, and then the main room with a low round platform in the middle as hearth for an open fire. Four columns supported the roof, and a throne was set against the wall on the right. Behind the main defensive wall, which was topped with battlements, were the palace storerooms. The citadel had two entrances, one of which was the Lion Gate – hidden from view here by the jutting tower on its right. Nearby, the walls bulge out to enclose the Grave Circle, a royal cemetery of an earlier date. Outside the walls lay another grave circle, beehive tombs, and houses.

Right: A reconstruction of the Lion Gate, seen already in Schliemann's view on the previous page. Battlements crest the walls and doors fill the open gateway. The gate is set back at the end of an open "tunnel", so that attackers could be pelted with arrows and spears from the battlements on both sides. The stonework of the gateway and side walls shows the careful cutting and fitting of the huge stone blocks, which made them strong as well as very impressive-looking. In other parts of the citadel's defenses, the rough boulder style called Cyclopean is more common.

Right: A plan of the citadel corresponding with the view above. The fortification wall generally follows the contours of the rocky hill, using its natural defenses, but veers out to enclose the "holy ground" of the earlier Grave Circle, and to form the "trap" in front of the Lion Gate and a semi-overlap at the North Postern Gate. At the top, a later extension was built to enclose a secret underground water-supply, with steps cut into the rock leading to it. This was essential in times of siege.

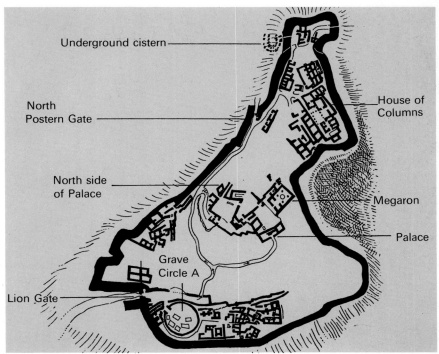

Underground cistern

North Postern Gate

North side of Palace

Grave Circle A

Lion Gate

House of Columns

Megaron

Palace

Tombs and Other Citadels

The nine beehive tombs at Mycenae vary in size and style, and have been dated from 1500 to 1300 BC. Their doorways are made of large stone slabs, sometimes with decorated half-columns on either side and a carved slab filling the triangular space over the lintel, as in the Lion Gate. The earlier tombs had domed chambers and entranceways built of rubble; in the later ones, built of finest ashlar or squared stone, the domes were decorated with bronze plates or rosettes. The dead were buried in pits, either in the main chamber or a smaller side one. Simpler tombs hollowed out of the hillside have also been discovered. They are squarish cells with shorter entrances, and were the family vaults of nobles and rich citizens. Some contained grave goods – weapons, tools, jewelery and pots – left as a tribute to the dead, or as objects to be used in after life.

Beehive and chamber tombs have been found in other parts of Greece. Some had already been robbed by the time the archaeologists arrived, but others brought to light some remarkable objects. One contained body-armor made of bronze plates and helmets covered with boars' tusks. In another, horses had been ceremonially buried in the entrance. The side chamber roof of a third was a massive slab entirely carved with linked spirals; a fourth was oval in shape like an upturned boat. Where beehive tombs exist, they suggest the presence nearby of some princely seat, for only local rulers would have been likely to control the resources needed to build them.

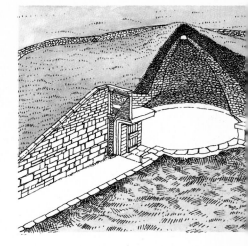

Above: A view of the inside of a beehive tomb, one of the royal family burial chambers at Mycenae. Inside is the round, underground chamber, the *tholos*. Its dome-like roof was lined with stones and covered by a mound of earth and stones. The dead were buried in pits in the *tholos* or in the side chamber. Between burials, the entry-passage was filled with earth.

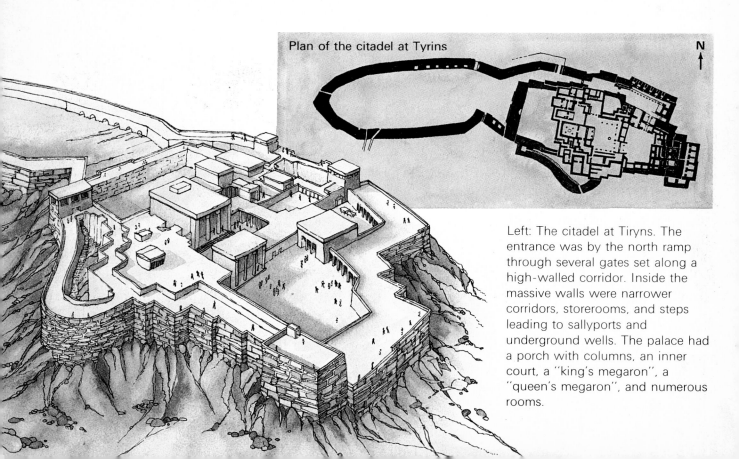

Plan of the citadel at Tyrins

N ↑

Left: The citadel at Tiryns. The entrance was by the north ramp through several gates set along a high-walled corridor. Inside the massive walls were narrower corridors, storerooms, and steps leading to sallyports and underground wells. The palace had a porch with columns, an inner court, a "king's megaron", a "queen's megaron", and numerous rooms.

There are other Mycenaean citadels at Tiryns, Argos, Nauplion, Athens, Thebes and Gla, similar to Mycenae in siting, appearance, and their "Cyclopean" boulder-built defenses. This points to a common level of culture and political organization throughout much of southern Greece in the late Bronze Age. But the term Mycenaean is used to describe the period as a whole because of the obvious wealth of Mycenae, its importance in later legend, and because it was the first site to be excavated.

The citadels were probably the centers of small kingdoms, perhaps at times in alliance, at times in conflict. Their massive defenses suggest that the people of the time lived in a state of armed tension and threatening war. The secret underground fountains added in certain citadels emphasize this, and there is also evidence of assault, destruction, fire, and total or temporary abandonment. When Mycenaean civilization collapsed or decayed, the citadels lost their old importance.

But the great ruins which amazed later Greeks remained and kindled the imagination of their poets and painters. Half-remembered history was distilled into legends: tales of Perseus and Pelops, the founders of two Mycenaean dynasties; of King Agamemnon who led a Greek army to conquer Troy; of the hero Achilles who killed the Trojan champion Hector; and of the hero Odysseus' return from Troy to Ithaca. No-one retold these tales better than Homer. His great poems, the *Iliad* and the *Odyssey*, now about 2700 years old, profoundly influenced Greeks of archaic and classical times, and also inspired Schliemann to search for "Mycenae, rich in gold".

Above: Little is known about the Greek poet Homer, yet his long epic poems, the *Iliad* and the *Odyssey*, are two of the greatest works of literature ever written. Several Greek cities claimed to have been his birthplace, his home, or his burial place. One of these, the island state of Ios, issued this coin, with its imaginary portrait of Homer, in the 4th century BC.

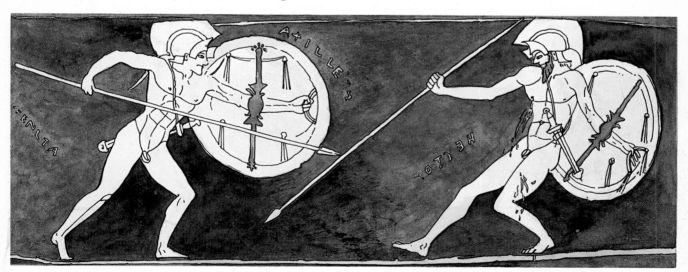

Above: Greek artists would often portray scenes from Homer's poems and other heroic tales in sculpture on stone, in molded terracota, on metalwork, and on

Here a red-figure vase from the 5th century BC shows one of the most dramatic events in Homer's *Iliad*: the duel to the death between the heroes Achilles and Hector.

Ancient Greek warriors would normally have worn bronze armor in battle, but classical artists often showed the Greek heroes fighting naked as they are on the vase.

Athens

Northward from Mycenae, across the bridge of land called the Isthmus which separates central and southern Greece, lies the city of Athens. Athens was Greece's most famous *polis* or city-state, the typical political unit in Greece in archaic and classical times.

Athens, with its own Mycenaean past and legends, had, by the 5th century BC, become a very powerful city and the center of an empire. We know a great deal about it from written evidence left by Athenians and others, and archaeologists have added to that. The people of Athens contributed more than most to Greek literature and art, and even after Athens lost political leadership, it remained a center of culture.

In order to survive, a *polis* needed to be able to defend itself, to be independent and to be prosperous. Athens had its own fortress, the Acropolis or "high city", rising from the plain like an island above a sea of houses. It has often been garrisoned by soldiers protecting or policing the citizens living below, and has often been bravely defended. To the west, the city walls curved over a line of hills, providing vantage points for the defence of the city.

Enclosed by mountains, the plain of Athens forms a self-contained unit in the Attica peninsula. However, legend told that Attica had been united under Athenian rule from the early days when Theseus was king. The state of Athens then included not only the city and its home plain, but the whole peninsula. Its greater size gave it many advantages and, because the area is screened from the Isthmus by mountains, it was partly protected from passing invaders.

The Athenians claimed that King Theseus was a founder of their democracy – a system of government by the people in which all male citizens took part, either by voting directly on certain matters, or by electing others to represent them. Theseus did not really introduce democracy, but by unifying Attica and bringing peace, he turned warriors into citizens and made more regular government possible.

There were kings long after Theseus, but the government eventually changed to aristocracy or rule by the nobles. Some of these are remembered as law-givers, such as the severe Draco (621 BC) or the wise Solon (594 BC). Later came a period of tyranny (561–510 BC), when the nobleman Pisistratus seized power for himself and his family. In 508 BC, Cleisthenes reformed the constitution, and full democracy developed during the 5th and 4th centuries BC. By that time, all male citizens could vote and hold positions of power.

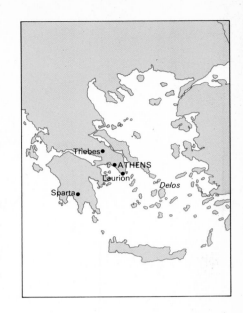

Ostraca

Voting disks

Above: These small finds are evidence of two ways in which Athenian citizens shared in the running of their city. Ostraca are fragments of broken pots on which citizens scratched the name of any official or politician they disapproved of. A majority vote of this kind against a person meant banishment from the city for ten years. The metal voting disks were used by juries to vote "guilty" or "not guilty" in trials.

In Mycenaean times, the Acropolis was the citadel of the kings of Athens. Parts of its fortress wall can still be seen, and a staircase to an underground spring has been discovered. Later, the rock remained the seat of power for kings and would-be rulers: the nobleman Cylon seized it in 632 BC in his unsuccessful attempt at sole rule or tyranny, and the successful Pisistratus kept it under his control. Its religious importance grew as larger temples were built, especially those dedicated to Athena, the goddess of the city. When the Persians captured Athens in 480 BC, they overcame a desperate defense of the Acropolis by the temple priests and those too poor to afford safe passage elsewhere. All the temples were destroyed.

The Acropolis was completely replanned in the 5th century BC. In 467–462 BC a new defensive wall was built around the summit, which provided a larger level area for building. Temples and other structures were built in more magnificent style in a program started by the popular leader Pericles to beautify Athens and give work to the citizens. Athena's new temple, the Parthenon (447–432 BC), the Propylaea (437–432 BC), the small temple of Athena the Victorious (420s BC), and the Erechtheum (421–407 BC) still stand. Meanwhile civic and commercial life flourished in the Agora or public square in the lower city, in the area which was known as the Ceramicus or Potters' Quarter.

Above: The Acropolis, the "high city" of Athens, was originally a fortress with a king's palace. In the classical period, it became the civil and religious center of the city. This reconstructed view from the northwest shows its Propylaea or "fore-gates", the Parthenon or main temple of the patron goddess Athena, and the Erechtheum temple with side porches.

An Athenian vase of the classical period

The Agora

This reconstruction of the ancient Agora or public square of Athens is seen from the north, looking towards the Acropolis hill. The view is partly based on evidence visible above ground since ancient times, such as the Parthenon and the other buildings on the Acropolis and the temple in the lower right of the picture. This so-called Temple of Theseus (more correctly "of Hephaistos") is the best preserved temple in Athens, indeed in all Greece. More evidence came from a half-century of large-scale excavations by American archaeologists. They removed houses and shops of recent times and revealed the area which had once been the open meeting place, the sacred and public buildings in it, and several private houses around its edges. The Agora started, in the 7th century BC, as a public square with very modest buildings, mainly on the west (right). Small stone pillars were added at street-corners to mark its boundaries. By the late 5th century, it looked much as it does here. Below is a drawing of the Agora as it was nearly 700 years later, as the travel writer Pausanias described it in the 2nd century AD. Many fine Hellenistic and Roman buildings had been added, and it is possible to give names to many of them from his book.

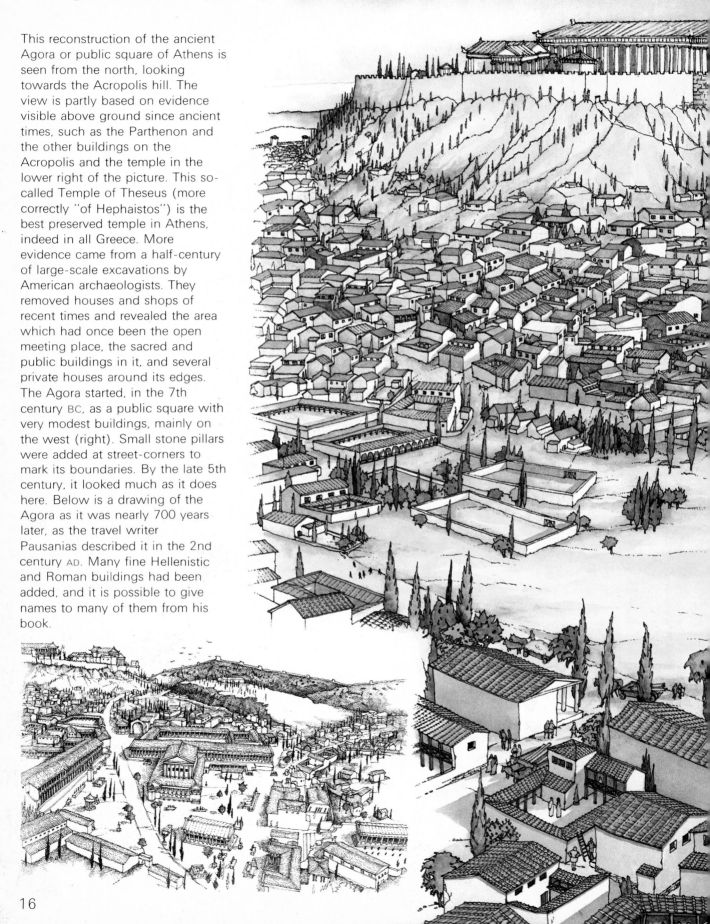

Athens

The City at War

The survival and prosperity of Athens in the 5th century BC depended on its sea-power, on its fleet of war galleys or triremes and on the trade of its merchant ships. When the Persians first invaded Greece in 490 BC, they sailed across the Aegean Sea and landed in northeastern Attica, at Marathon. The Athenian hoplites – the heavily-armed citizen soldiers – defeated them there in a land battle. Our Marathon races today commemorate the achievement of an Athenian athlete, Pheidippides, who ran all the way from Marathon to Athens (about 25 miles) with the glad news of victory. By the time the Persians attacked again in 480 BC, the Athenians, urged on by their far-sighted leader, Themistocles, had built their largest ever fleet. Its two hundred galleys defeated the Persians at the battle of Salamis.

The Persians were at last expelled from Greece by a war-alliance between the Spartans, the Athenians and other Greeks. Athens then took the lead in liberating the Greeks of the Aegean islands and the coastal cities of Asia Minor. A league was formed, centered on the island of Delos, to ensure their common liberty, but Athens turned this league into an Athenian empire. The other city-states, Corinth, Sparta and Thebes, felt threatened and war finally broke out. The Peloponnesian War, which lasted from 431 to 404 BC, ended in defeat of Athens and the destruction of her empire.

The power of Athens in the 5th century BC depended largely on her fleet of fighting galleys or triremes – the name being derived from words for "three" and "oars", and meaning "three-banker". Above and below left are representations of a sailing ship from a vase and an oared galley from a fragment of sculpture.

Below, a reconstruction of an Athenian trireme approaching the port of Piraeus, with Athens itself in the distance.

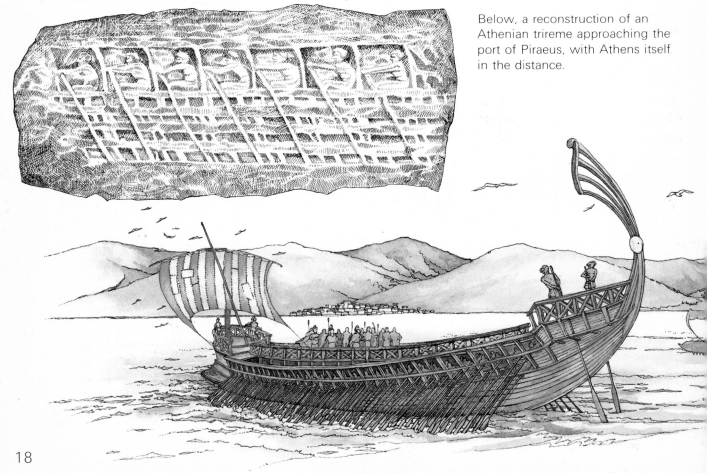

When the Athenians enlarged their fleet from 483 BC onwards, they needed safe harbors, naval dockyards, and all the facilities of a port. Earlier, they had been content with beaching their ships at Phaleron Bay to prevent the wooden hulls becoming waterlogged and slow to handle. But the long bay was open to attack. In 493 BC, Themistocles began to develop the Piraeus promontory as a naval port, fortifying the large northern harbor, Kantharos, and the two small enclosed southern basins, Zea and Munychia. In about 450 BC, straight new streets and rectangular blocks for public buildings and houses were laid out at Piraeus, on a much more regular plan than in old Athens. At the east end, a hill served as a local "acropolis", and strong walls guarded against land attacks. Themistocles had advised the Athenians to abandon the old city and remove to Piraeus, defend its walls, equip their ships, control the seas and the trade routes, and defy all enemies.

Instead, the Athenians built long walls joining Athens to Piraeus and Phaleron (461–456 BC) and then added a third wall in 455 BC which formed a narrow corridor, five miles long, between the old city and Piraeus, along which men and supplies could move safely. Athens could not be surrounded nor, as long as her fleet guarded the supply route from the cornfields of the Black Sea coast, could she be starved into surrender.

When the Peloponnesian War started, the people living out in the country were sheltered in the city and pitched battles with the well-drilled Spartan army were avoided. In 430 BC, plague broke out, destroying a quarter of the population. Yet Athens held out until, 25 years later, her fleet was captured in a surprise attack, while the crews were on shore. Piraeus was blockaded and Athens surrendered. To the sound of Spartan pipes, the Long Walls and the city walls were demolished.

Above: Excavated remains, now re-buried, of ship-sheds at Zea harbor, Piraeus. These sheds housed the triremes when they were not in use. Below: a plan of the harbor town, Piraeus, and the upper city of Athens. Piraeus, built up only in the 5th century BC, was given a regular grid-plan, but the old city, four miles inland, had an irregular street plan centered on the Acropolis. The long walls between them formed a fortified corridor which meant that, as long as she controlled the seas, Athens could withstand siege.

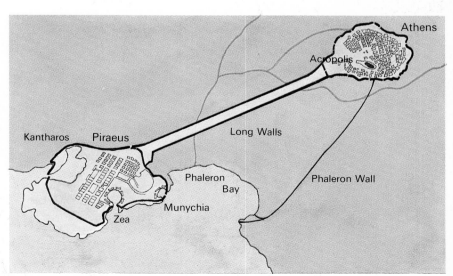

Living in Athens

While soldiers and statesmen held the stage in the city of Athens, there is also evidence of how ordinary people lived behind the scenes, and how the city's wealth was produced. Rough underground caves have been discovered outside the city, dedicated to the country god Pan and to the Nymphs, which starkly contrast with the splendid marble temples on the Acropolis. The worship of Pan, god of the shepherds of the Peloponnese, had spread in Attica after the Marathon campaign in 490 BC. Caves on mountain-sides were dedicated to him, like the one near Marathon itself and another south of Athens at Vari.

Themistocles' mighty fleet, which brought Athens its imperial power, was paid for by the vast profits from a lucky strike of rich ore in the silver mines at Laurion in southernmost Attica. There, far from the public eye and even the light of day, worked thousands of slaves and hundreds of free men. The forested hills are today full of traces of their industry: galleries and caverns where lead-miners tunneled by the light of oil lamps with hammers and chisels very like those in Archidamus' hands. On the surface are the remains of workshops. Here silver-rich lead ore was ground small, and washed in flowing water to separate the heavy ore from the lighter stony dust. The ore was sent to furnaces for smelting, and the lead was then separated from the precious silver, which was minted into coins in Athens.

Above: The Cave of Pan near Vari south of Athens. This carving in the rock, perhaps a self-portrait, is of a certain Archidamus who decorated the cave with sculptures and inscriptions.

Above: The preserved remains of a large ore-washery at Agrileza in the ancient silver-mining area of Attica. This view shows its wide cemented floor, a round pit and channels, and a row of three column-bases at the back.
Left: A reconstruction of the same washery with its shed roof cut away to show the water tank and the washing floor with its sloping wooden troughs. The water channels and sedimentation basins are set around the larger drying floor. Several ore washeries have recently been excavated; the one illustrated here, dating from the 4th century BC, was cleared by the author.

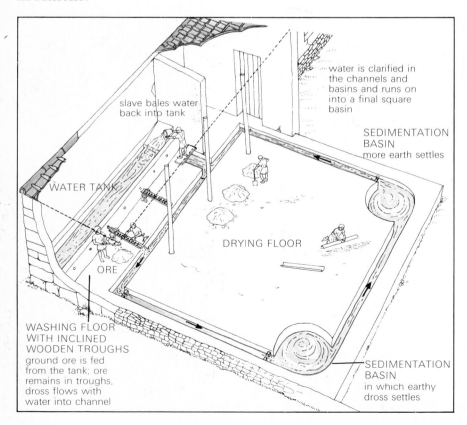

slave bales water back into tank

water is clarified in the channels and basins and runs on into a final square basin

SEDIMENTATION BASIN
more earth settles

WATER TANK

DRYING FLOOR

ORE

WASHING FLOOR WITH INCLINED WOODEN TROUGHS
ground ore is fed from the tank; ore remains in troughs, dross flows with water into channel

SEDIMENTATION BASIN
in which earthy dross settles

The houses of the ordinary citizens of Athens and the irregular streets contrasted oddly with the magnificence of the temples, according to a visitor in the 3rd century BC. American excavators have uncovered several houses around the fringes of the Agora. One at the southwest corner occupied an awkward plot between two alleys. Objects found there suggest it was a cobbler's house and workshop. Nearby at the foot of Pnyx Hill, other houses have been excavated by Greek archaeologists. One, deeply terraced into the steep hillside, had leveled floors and standing walls of solid rock, carried upwards in mud brick.

Out in the countryside, the author and two friends have excavated a 5th century BC farmhouse near the so-called Dema frontier-wall northwest of Athens, and also a 4th century BC house at Vari not far from the Cave of Pan. Both were rectangular, well-built houses, set square and level on spacious sites, unlike the cramped plots in the oldest parts of Athens. Such were the homes of the craftsmen and peasant farmers who made up the free citizens of ancient Athens.

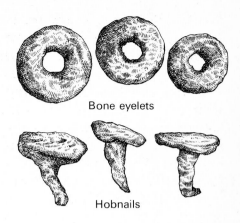

Bone eyelets

Hobnails

Above: Evidence of a cobbler's trade. The bone eyelets for lace-holes and the hobnails for the soles of sandals were found in one of the houses reconstructed below, identified by the name on a cup base as the House of Simon.

Left: In this corner house off the Agora, Simon the cobbler may have lived, a friend of the philosopher Socrates. Note the Agora boundary stone embedded right at the angle of the house.

Right: On Pnyx Hill in Athens, some house remains have been found on either side of a steep alleyway. They show that the rooms were cut deep into the hillside with boldly projecting partition walls. One such house is reconstructed here.

Left: A farmhouse sited near the Dema Wall, a frontier defense in northwest Attica. Low rubble foundations for mud-brick walls and some fragments of tiles have survived which provide evidence for this reconstruction.

Right: A rather smaller farmhouse sited on a ridge downhill from the Cave of Pan near Vari. It had an internal courtyard paved with flagstones, and a thick-walled corner room probably built up high as a store-tower.

Olympia

The great sanctuary at Olympia was sacred to Zeus, whom Homer called the "Father of Gods and Men". It was open to all free-born Greeks to visit in peace, to worship the god and celebrate his festival.

Zeus was the head of the Olympian family of gods and goddesses worshiped in Greece in archaic and classical times. Their name Olympian came from Mount Olympus in Thessaly, the highest peak in Greece, where Zeus was said to live enthroned above the clouds with his wife Hera and the other gods. Although other places, such as Dodona and Nemea, were sacred to Zeus, it was at Olympia that the most important festival was held in his honor. The Olympic Games, athletic contests which took place during the festival, became famous throughout Greece. There were others too: the Nemean Games in honor of Zeus, the sea-god Poseidon's Isthmian Games near Corinth, and the Pythian Games at Delphi in honor of Apollo. To win at any of these was an athlete's supreme ambition. The prize was only a leafy crown – of wild olive at Olympia, wild celery at Nemea and Isthmia, and bay-leaves at Delphi – but the real reward was the glory of victory.

Below: Olympia as viewed from near the end of the raised Terrace of the Treasuries, looking eastward along the full length of the Stadium. (See if you can find this view on the plan at the top of the opposite page.)

Below: A view of the Palaestra or wrestling school used for exercise, contests and relaxation. It was planned as a large open courtyard enclosed by roofed colonnades and rooms of various sizes, now marked by re-erected columns and stone wall-slabs.

1. Stadium
2. Treasuries
3. Temple of Hera
4. Tomb of Pelops
5. Altar of Zeus
6. Temple of Zeus
7. Philippeion
8. Council House
9. Palaestra
10. Gymnasion
11. Leonidaion
12. Baths

- Archaic
- Classical
- Hellenistic
- Roman

Above: A plan of the festival center at Olympia, as it has so far been excavated. It shows how buildings were added or rebuilt over the centuries, and the main periods are shown by the different colors.

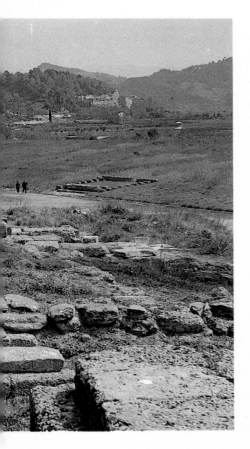

The sanctuary of Zeus was a sacred grove of trees called the Altis. It lay on the level plain between the rivers Alpheus and Cladeus and was bounded on three sides by a wall and on the north by the Hill of Cronus, named after the father of Zeus. The area had been sacred in the Bronze Age, even before Zeus had taken over this sanctuary, when a cleft or small cave in the Hill of Cronus was regarded as a place of prophecy or an oracle of Ge, Mother Earth. Only a few traces of small buildings within the Altis have been excavated as evidence of this earliest period of use. Also within the Altis was an earth mound honored as the Tomb of Pelops, the hero after whom the Peloponnese ("Island of Pelops") was named. That mound was later enclosed by a wall which made it a small fenced grove within the Altis.

From the 10th to the 7th centuries BC, the worship of Zeus and the other gods was carried on almost entirely in the open air. There was a large altar made of earth and ash for Zeus and smaller altars for Hera and the Mother of the Gods. In the late 7th and 6th centuries several buildings were added: the Temple of Hera in the northeast corner of the Altis, a Prytaneum or official home for the priests and presidents of the festival, and Treasuries built by various cities. To the south, outside the Altis, a Council House was built.

In the 5th century BC, a massive stone temple was erected for Zeus himself, and more buildings, particularly colonnades or stoas, were added along the edges of the Altis or outside it. Later the Altis itself was extended southward when a new boundary wall was built. In early days, the foot races were run from near the Altar of Zeus, but later the Stadium or racetrack was built farther east, a level area about 650 feet long with earth banks for the spectators and rows of seats half-way along for the judges.

The Sanctuary Buildings

A northward view of the sanctuary reconstructed from the remains uncovered over a hundred years of excavations. In early archaic times, there were only a few simple buildings. Many elaborate structures were added in classical times and, by the Roman period, Olympia looked much as it is shown below. The buildings on the left were outside the west wall of the sanctuary.

Below are the Gymnasion (exercise area); the square Palaestra (wrestling school) with shady colonnades, rooms and sanded court; the Bathhouse at its corner; the tall Workshop of Pheidias where the sculptor made the colossal statue of Zeus for the chief temple; and the Leonidaion or "hotel" for important visitors, also with its courtyard, colonnades and rooms.

The west boundary of the Altis or Sacred Grove had two walls, the inner Greek, the outer, with its south gate and extension, of Roman date. Inside are the round "temple" of King Philip of Macedon (with the Prytaneion or Officials' House behind it), the low tile-roofed Temple of Hera, and the mound-like Tomb of Pelops.

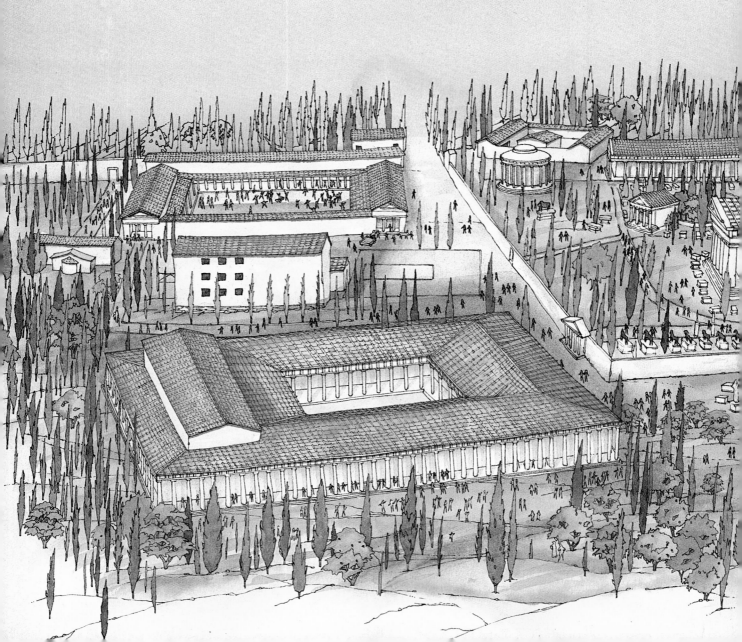

In the south of the Altis rose the high marble-roofed Temple of Zeus which contained a magnificent gold and ivory statue of the god. Outside the wall are the two round-ended halls of the Council House and the long South Colonnade.

Below, the conical Hill of Cronus overlooks the grove of Zeus. At its foot stand the half-round fountain-house of Herodus Atticus, the long row of Treasuries which front onto the Altis, and the small temple of the Mother of the Gods.

The east side of the sanctuary was closed by the Echo Colonnade and the colonnaded Judges' Hall. Beyond lies the Stadium or running track, with its banked sides and stone starting-lines. Eventually the whole sanctuary was damaged by serious earthquakes and floods, and covered in deep mud brought down by rain and the rivers.

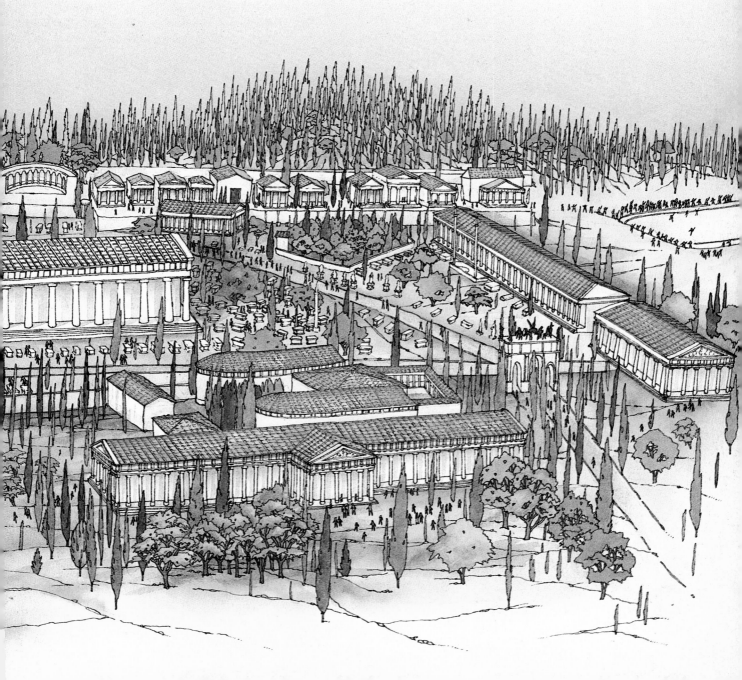

The Temples

Our evidence about Olympia itself comes from two main sources. One is the travel-book of Pausanias who visited Olympia in Roman times, in the 2nd century AD, and left descriptions of the buildings and statues, the ceremonies and the games. The other are the ruins themselves as revealed by excavation. In 1829 a French expedition recovered some of the sculptures from the Temple of Zeus which are now exhibited in Paris. Large-scale excavations were started between 1875 and 1881 by German archaeologists, and work there has continued at intervals ever since. There are now visible remains of buildings which had been destroyed by earthquakes in late Roman times and still later covered over by deep mud when the rivers changed their courses. The ancient descriptions helped the archaeologists to identify and restore in drawings and models most of the main buildings, particularly the temples of Hera and Zeus which Pausanias described in detail.

The Temple of Hera is one of the oldest known Greek temples, and the remains seen today are those of the third temple on this very site. Built around 600 BC, it was in use for about 1000 years. Parts of the walls and columns have been re-erected on its foundation platform. The walls were of stone blocks in their lower parts and of sun-dried bricks above, while the columns, originally of wood were rebuilt in stone as need arose and so vary in style. Pausanias himself saw one of the wooden columns and also described the old-fashioned statue of Hera, enthroned, with Zeus standing at her side. Only the base of this remains, and what may be the head of the goddess herself, shown in the photograph above.

Above: This early archaic sculptured head of the goddess Hera was found between the Temple of Hera and the Palaestra. Made of stone, in about 600 BC, it was probably from the temple, and may have belonged to a statue of Hera enthroned, which the Roman travel-writer Pausanias described as of "simple style".

The Temple of Hera, built in the early 6th century BC, is one of the oldest surviving Greek temples. The view right shows how repairs over the centuries have left it with columns of different dates, made of varying numbers of blocks. The reconstruction below shows its low profile.

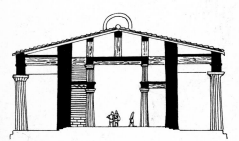

The Temple of Zeus was built much later than that of Hera, about 465–456 BC, and it was far larger and grander. The walls and columns were of local stone covered with fine plaster which had a white marble finish, and the roof was covered with marble tiles. In the ancient style, parts of the columns and the decorative panels above them were painted in bright reds and blues, while golden shields were added later. The two pediments or low triangular spaces at the gable-ends were filled with sculptured figures, larger than life size. The east or front pediment depicts the start of the legendary chariot race between the hero Pelops and the local king Oenomaus. In the center stands Zeus himself, the supreme judge. On his left are Oenomaus and his queen, on his right Pelops and the king's daughter Hippodameia; her hand in marriage was the prize of victory, but death was the forfeit if Pelops lost. Next came chariots and horses, and the kneeling and seated figures of charioteers, grooms, hand-maidens, and seers or prophets. On the west pediment is a more violent scene. The god Apollo in the center brings order to another mythical struggle; men battle against centaurs – half-men, half-horses – who tried to carry off the women from a wedding feast. Inside the temple once stood one of the wonders of the ancient world – the huge statue of Zeus enthroned in majesty, covered in gold and ivory.

Above: The head of the seer or prophet Iamos, part of the free-standing group of marble figures of more than life size which filled the east pediment of the Temple of Zeus. He looks worried, perhaps foreseeing that King Oenomaus would die in an "accident" arranged by the Wily Pelops.

Above: The temple of Zeus in ruins with its huge columns toppled by earthquakes. Right: This reconstruction shows how the temple looked in classical times, with the outer columns, the walls, and the inner rows of smaller columns set on larger ones. The great statue of Zeus enthroned was of gold and ivory. Below are the sculptural groups which decorated the gable-end pediments.

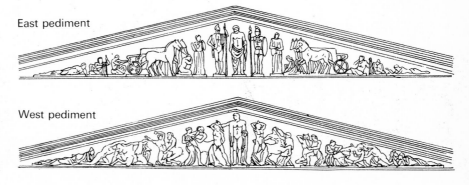

East pediment

West pediment

The Games

Above: The starting line in the Stadium. A line of stones embedded at each end of the running track marked the start and end of the foot-races. Parallel grooves cut in the stones gave the runners a better grip for their feet and posts set in the starting line marked the position of each runner.

Olympia is particularly famous for those ancient games which inspired the ideal and some of the practices of the modern Olympic Games. The modern games, held only since 1896, take place every four years, like the ancient Olympics. The Greeks, who had no common system of dating years, used the celebration of each Olympiad as a rough means of dating. The first official Olympiad took place as early as 776 BC, and the games were held, with a few rare irregularities, until at least AD 393 – that is for over 1100 years. As the Greeks were often at war, it became their practice to arrange a truce for a month or, later, three months to allow the festival and games to be held. Only free-born citizens of Greek descent were allowed to compete, till Greece became part of the Roman Empire, when Roman citizens were accepted as competitors. By then also the general peace which Roman rule brought to Greek lands meant that there was no need to arrange special truces.

At first all events were exclusively for men. For 50 years, the only contest was the foot-race – a long sprint run over a length of one stade, or nearly 200 metres. That race determined the length of the stadium. In 724 and 720 BC two more races were added – the *diaulos* or double-stade, when runners ran once up and down the stadium, and the *dolichos* or 24 lengths of the stadium, and so a long-distance race rather like the modern 5000 metres. In these, the runners had to make a sharp turn round a post, whereas modern athletes run round the gentle curves of an oval race-track.

Right: These three athletes are involved in three of the five events of the Greek pentathlon – from left to right: discus, javelin and the foot-race. The runner is in the ancient starting position, a standing-crouch, as implied by the close-set grooves of the starting lines. Greek artists loved to use athletes as models, portraying them nude as they were during the real contests.

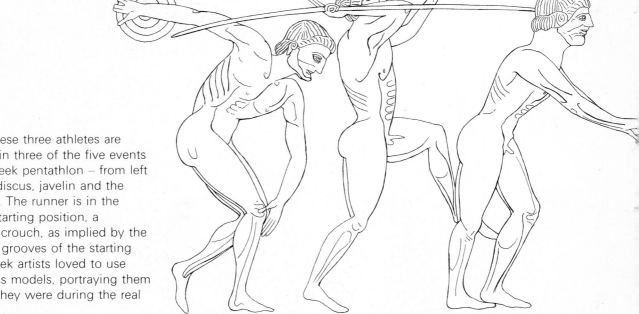

28

Little by little, more events were added to the Games. As well as wrestling, boxing, chariot racing, the *pankration* or unarmed combat, and horse racing, there was the *pentathlon* – a five-event contest which included discus, long jump, javelin, running and wrestling. In 632 BC boys' events came in: the foot-race, wrestling and, later, boxing. A men's foot-race in armor was introduced in 520 BC. Later changes mainly involved races for mares, mules and colts, ridden bareback or pulling chariots, which took place in the hippodrome, a much longer track south of the stadium. Girls' races formed part of a separate four-yearly festival of Hera.

The race in armor and the peace truces remind us that war was only too common in ancient Greece. The many bronze helmets, shields, cuirasses, and greaves or leg-armor, dedicated as trophies to Zeus, and found at Olympia, are also evidence of this.

Below: Greek citizen-soldiers of classical times arming for battle – a view based on evidence from statuettes and vases of the time. These foot-soldiers are putting on full armor: bronze helmets with horsehair crests; breastplates of leather or thick linen made in a waistcoat shape with shoulder-pieces and waist-flaps; bronze greaves for the shins; and large round shields.

Two helmets found at Olympia in recent years, both once dedicated as memorials of military victories.

Delos

Delos is the most central of the Cycladic islands in the Aegean Sea, and one of the smallest. In antiquity it was of great importance first as a sanctuary of Apollo and a center of pilgrimage, and later as one of the greatest commercial ports of the Mediterranean.

Delos is today a town of ruins set on an uninhabited, treeless island in a blue sea – an island which appears fresh and green in spring, but which in summer is hot, dry and dusty. The Greek historian Thucydides wrote that its first settlers were pirates from Caria in Asia Minor, who were then driven away when King Minos of Crete gained control of the Aegean Sea. Greeks from the mainland had colonized the island before 1000 BC. By the 8th century BC, Delos, the supposed birthplace of the god Apollo and his sister Artemis, was already considered holy.

During the archaic period, the most important buildings were those of Apollo's sanctuary. Pilgrims probably landed at a northerly bay and walked south along a processional path. On their left lay the oval Sacred Lake and the Garden of Leto, mother of Apollo and Artemis. On their right was the Terrace of Lions, a row of nine or more male lions carved in gleaming white Naxian marble. Ahead was the Agora of the Twelve Gods and the sanctuary itself, a group of small temples and stoas dominated by a colossal statue of Apollo.

Above: One of the archaic sculptured lions which lined the earliest processional way to the Sanctuary of Apollo.
Below: The earliest pilgrims approached the sanctuary southward, down the Avenue of Lions. In archaic times, it was a small group of buildings with the Hall of the Naxians and the huge statue of Apollo at their center.

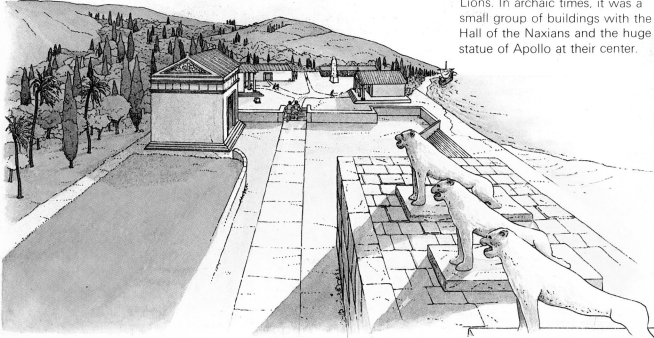

Delos escaped damage during the Persian Wars. Then in 478 BC it became the official center of the Delian League, an alliance of Aegean states dedicated to crusade against Persia. The allies paid tribute to a common treasury kept at Delos, but Athens transformed the league into an Athenian empire and removed the treasury to their Acropolis. In 426 BC the Athenians "purified" Delos by removing the remains of the dead to nearby Rheneia and in 422 they also expelled the living natives. The fall of the Athenian Empire in 404 interrupted this rule, but not for long. Athens regained indirect control and kept it till 314 BC. So throughout the classical period it was Athenian policy which decided how Delos developed. Some small buildings were added to the sanctuary, but the Great Temple, started in the early days of the Delian League, was not completed till Athens lost all control. However Athens dedicated one new temple, the Temple of the Athenians, shortly after the purification of Delos.

When Alexander the Great, king of Macedonia and conqueror of all Persia, died in 323 BC, his vast personal empire split up into kingdoms ruled by his generals. Three of these kingdoms, Macedonia, Syria and Egypt, dominated the Eastern Mediterranean until they were conquered by the Romans. In this so-called hellenistic period, Delos formed part of a league of islands "protected" first by Egypt, later by Macedonia. Evidence of their influence is clear in the new festivals named after royal Egyptians and the colonnades built by Macedonian kings.

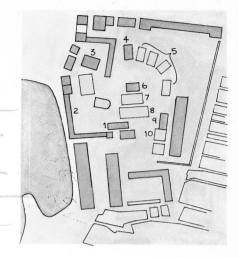

Above: A plan of the development of the Sanctuary. The buildings in red date from archaic times, those in blue were added in Classical times, and those in yellow in the later Hellenistic period. 1. Naxians' Hall 2. Naxian Stoa and annex 3. Temple of Artemis 4. archaic Treasury 5. classical Treasuries 6. Porinos Temple 7. Athenian Temple 8. Great Temple 9. Council House 10. Official Residence. Below: A northward view to the Hellenistic sanctuary.

The Port

The extensive excavations on Delos have provided enough evidence for architects and artists to attempt reconstruction models and pictures of both individual buildings and the general scene. On the far right, the author's photograph shows the ruins of the Sanctuary of Apollo and nearby parts of the ancient town, as well as the harbor and the straits between Delos and the island of Rheneia. Below is the artist's reconstruction from that same viewpoint.

The view is northwestwards from the slopes of Mount Cynthus, the central peak of the island. On the left are the houses and commercial buildings along the harbor. The many large buildings with courtyards and colonnades around the Sanctuary area were mostly added in the Hellenistic period. Many were built by royal or noble patrons of Delos, such as Antigonus Gonatas, King of Macedon, or Philip V of Macedon.

South of the Sanctuary was a business quarter with colonnaded arcades or Stoas (the West Stoa, the Stoa of Philip and the South Stoa) and an agora. East of the Sanctuary was a triangular-shaped extension formed by the long Monument of the Bulls (320 BC), the simple East Boundary Wall, and the wide Stoa of Antigonus (250 BC) with its two projecting wings. Behind that on the right is the square market of the Italians (110 BC).

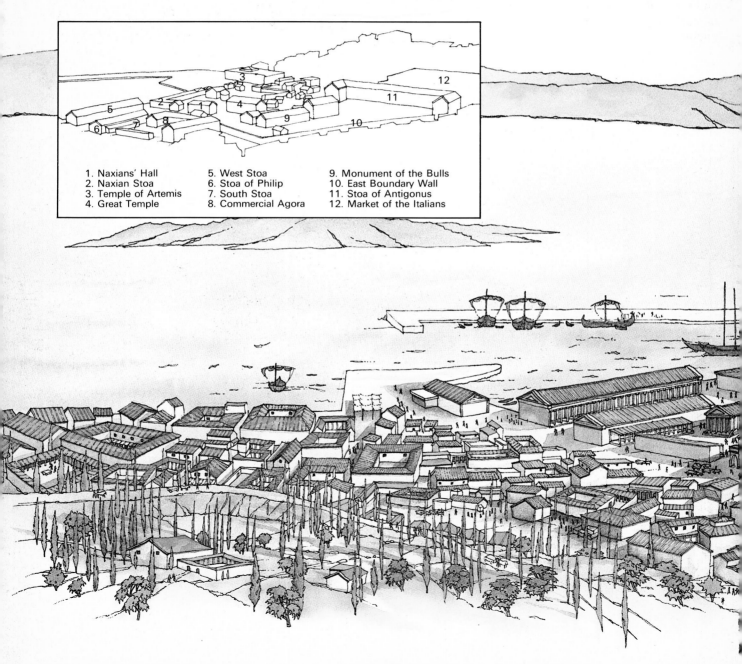

1. Naxians' Hall
2. Naxian Stoa
3. Temple of Artemis
4. Great Temple
5. West Stoa
6. Stoa of Philip
7. South Stoa
8. Commercial Agora
9. Monument of the Bulls
10. East Boundary Wall
11. Stoa of Antigonus
12. Market of the Italians

When Delos was ceremoniously purified in 426 BC, all tombs were opened and their contents reburied on Rheneia, the larger island visible across the straits. After that, no person was left to sicken and die on Delos. This early piety contrasts oddly with the inhumanity behind the commercial success of later Hellenistic Delos, when the island lived largely off its profits as the great slave-market of the Mediterranean. Delos became the seat of a bishop in early Christian times, but after various raids by pirates was abandoned in the later middle ages.

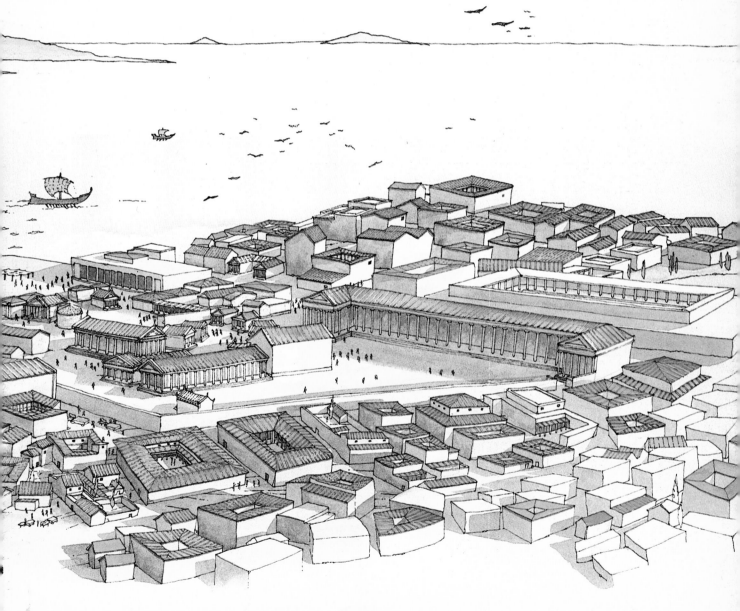

Merchants and Trade

In Hellenistic times, Delos prospered as a port, trading in corn bought and sold from elsewhere, and many foreign merchants settled there. Then came a sudden political change. In 166 BC the Romans, after conquering Macedonia, expelled the population of its ally Delos, gave the island to Athens to colonize with her own citizens, and declared it a free port. Their aim was mainly to undermine the flourishing trade of the island of Rhodes which had been too friendly towards Macedonia. As a free port, Delos attracted traders from all parts of the Mediterranean. Italians, Egyptians, Phoenicians, Jews, Syrians and Greeks together formed a thoroughly mixed, cosmopolitan population.

The town increased in size and the port was improved with offices and warehouses. A fine new commercial center, the Agora of the Italians, was built north of the sanctuary, and a great number of imposing new stone houses were built, with fine marble doorways, marble columns in their courtyards, and mosaic floors inside. The island lived on the import and export of goods from outside and a huge slave-trade dependent on Rome's many wars. In 88 BC Delos was raided by the navy of King Mithradates of Pontus in Asia Minor, an enemy of Rome, and again in 69 BC by his pirate allies who sacked the island. A century of prosperity ended almost as rapidly as it had started. No more fine mansions were built and the population dwindled, not merely because of those attacks but because direct trade began between Italy and the Near East and so cut out the middle-men of Delos.

Above: A view from the street of the ruins of a Hellenistic house on Delos, showing the stonework of its walls and main door. On this stony island, house walls were generally made of fairly small stones fitted together and plastered inside and out. The windows and doorways were often framed with marble slabs, as they are here. Inside the rooms, the wall plaster was sometimes lightly molded and painted in various colors to imitate formal bands and panels of large, carefully worked stones. The floors were either of cement, with panels of mosaic decoration made of small embedded pieces of colored stones, or entirely of mosaic. The mosaic was sometimes a formal and repetitive pattern, like the beautiful geometric floor on the left, sometimes more naturalistic, with human and animal figures or designs of leaves and flowers.

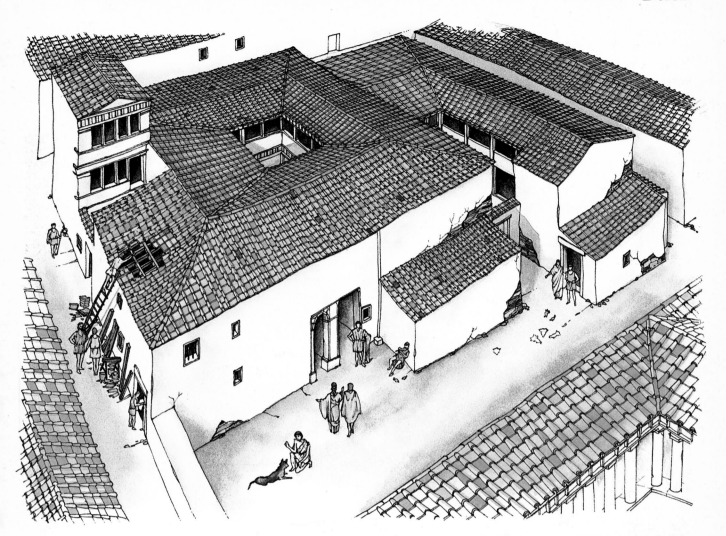

Above: An aerial reconstruction view of a block of three Hellenistic houses. On the left is the House of the Pediments, so called because of the decorative gable-ends of its tower; in the middle, the House of the Comedians, which has been given its name because of a fine wall painting which shows actors in the costumes of comedy and tragedy. To the right is the House of the Tritons, named after the mosaic of a mermaid-like sea creature – a Tritoness – on one of its floors. The tower belonging to the House of the Pediments, with its wide windows and pediments, was probably unusual, but inner courtyards were a common feature of Delian houses

The merchants left Delos for new markets; their houses fell into decay. Delos was no more than a village in Roman times; and gradually became a ghost town, finally abandoned and used only as a quarry for building stones.

In 1873 French archaeologists came to Delos to begin a century of excavation and study. They uncovered the robbed remains of the sanctuary's buildings, the colonnades and warehouses of the commercial quarter, public buildings like the theater, deep cisterns for rain-water, and large areas of paved streets and houses. Many houses still had painted plaster on their walls, and columns and door-posts lay where they had fallen, ready to be repaired and put back into position.

Now one can wander along quiet streets in the shade of house walls, look through stone-framed windows or pass through doorways into the homes of the long vanished merchants of the town, their courtyards paved with marble slabs and mosaics. The wealth of evidence provided by the ruins and finds enable the archaeologist and the artist to present a vivid picture of Delos in its century of greatest prosperity.

Glossary

ACROPOLIS: "high city", a citadel or hilltop fortress within a Greek city.

AGORA: an open area in a Greek city used as a market-place and public square.

ARCHAIC: old; old-fashioned. Used for an early style of Greek art before the classical period, and so for the period itself, about 800–500 BC.

BATTLEMENTS: the defenses along the top of a fortification wall.

BRONZE AGE: the long period when bronze (a mixture of copper and tin) was the main metal used for making tools in Greece, about 2500–1000 BC.

CISTERN: an underground store or source of water.

CITADEL: a fortified stronghold or refuge, often on a hill.

CITY-STATE: a city which, together with the surrounding district or region, formed an independent state.

CLASSICAL PERIOD: the period of city-state prosperity, about 500–300 BC. The word "classical" is used of Greek art and literature in the great age of city-states.

COLONIES: towns and cities founded outside the homeland.

CUIRASS: breastplate or armor for the upper part of the body, generally the breast, back and stomach.

DISCUS: a round, fairly flat disk to be held in one hand and thrown; used in throwing contests.

DYNASTY: a series of kings or rulers from the same family.

GREAVE: armor or guard for the shin or lower leg, from knee to ankle.

HELLENISTIC: a name derived from "Hellas" and "Hellenes" (the Greek names for Greece and Greeks). Used for the period following the classical period, from the conquests of Alexander the Great (336–323 BC) till the Roman conquest of Greece, so about 300–150 BC.

JAVELIN: a throwing spear.

MACEDONIA: a state ruled by a Greek dynasty in the north of Greece (now partly north Greece and partly southern Yugoslavia).

MOSAIC: a decorative floor covering for rooms and courtyards, made by embedding colored pebbles or small cut pieces of colored stone or glass in cement to form patterns and pictures.

MYCENAEAN AGE: a name for the later part of the Bronze Age, derived from that of Mycenae.

PENINSULA: an area of land almost surrounded by sea.

PANKRATION: an "all-in" contest; a form of all-in wrestling or unarmed combat combining wrestling and boxing.

PENTATHLON: a five-event athletic contest combining discus, javelin, wrestling, long-jumping (from a standing start), and a foot-race.

POLIS: the Greek name for a town or city, extended in the classical period to mean also the whole city-state.

SALLYPORT: a narrow gateway in a city wall; from "to sally", to rush out suddenly against an enemy.

SANCTUARY: a sacred area given over to religious worship; often enclosed by a fence or wall and containing temples.

STADIUM: a running track or sports ground; its name and length come from the "stade" – a Greek measure just under 200 metres long.

STOA: the Greek name for a long building, walled in at the back and sides but open along the front, where there was a row of columns to support the upper floor or the roof; a colonnade; a portico.

TYRANT: a single ruler of a state who was not king by right, but obtained and kept power by popular support or even by force of arms.

Index